HOW TO FLOW WITH WITH LAW OF ATTRACTION

JOANNE LOWEY

ISBN:1519311362
ISBN-13:9781519311368

DEDICATION

My thoughts are with my Mum and Dad for being survivors and not victims of circumstance. Furthermore, my extreme gratitude goes to my Dad who continues to inspire me with his determination and courage to live life to the full by not allowing his disability to prevent him from enjoying his life.

Whilst in the process of writing this manuscript, I was informed by people within our local community that my Father's experience following the consequences of his accident encourages others, and his account is often shared with moments of inspiration in them.

Whilst discussing family, l wish to thank my brother Tony for being you and my two sons Scott and Steven for putting up with my preaching on positivity and their eventual faith in me. I am so proud of how you both have grown that has been reinforced by my parents that makes me so overwhelmed with positive emotion.

Lastly, thanks to my partner Scott for providing us with our lifestyle that I love so much! I love each and every one of you with all of my heart!

Thank you thank you thank you!.

CONTENTS

ACKNOWLEDGMENTS

I wish to first thank our ancestors for attracting the law of attraction to me at a time in my life that I appreciated embarking on becoming a dedicated student.

l thank the wisdom of our ancestors for the discovery of the emerald tablet that explains the secret to a successful life is through inner work which I owe gratitude for.

In thanking many of mentors and law of attraction coaches, thank you Joe Vulgarmore, who was tolerant enough to help me on a one to one basis when I requested advice and in addition, would highly recommend Joe's book "Alignment" for anyone wishing to embark on their law of attraction journey.

Thank you to Joey McPhilips and Marilyn Holzmann. So much gratitude to Rhonda Byrne for the creation of 'THE SECRET' that I continue to watch over and over again and still, new information jumps out to me on each occasion.

Much appreciation to Esther and Jerry Hicks whose wisdom and true intentions to share on-line, workshops and groups, their knowledge and law of attraction tools that has aided me in my development.

l wish to thank my co-creating partner Diane Carle who I adore and greatly appreciate for sharing our journey, visualisations and assisted me in maintaining momentum and positive vibrations. I look forward to collaborating with you in the creation of further visualisation in the very near future - you are the sister I never had.

Thanks to Bob Lowey for your assistance in editing my book l am so grateful for your connection and offer of support.

·

INTRODUCTION

The intention of this manuscript is to share with you my journey through self awareness and mindfulness.

Hopefully, this may lead to supporting anyone through their life's progress that may even result in embarking on a magical journey where you may find your life's purpose, your true passions and possibly enabling you to write your own story.

I will share my knowledge of working with the universe in harmony through the law of attraction and cosmic ordering.

Step by step, like an instruction manual, this is for your own reference, whenever you need, and with each positive intention your confidence will grow.

As a unique individual, I hope you will experience co creating, the constructive resolution of conflicts or dilemmas that arise that will enable you to flourish and live the good life within the universe while enjoying your journey as you deserve it!

1 THE LAW OF ATTRACTION

If you have stumbled upon this book, it's not by coincidence!

My aim is to exercise the law of attraction to you! When you are ready to use this to your advantage through raising awareness, you may find that you are a perfect being who deserves a better life.

The law of attraction is a proven science. Science explains that our universe is made of energy, matter and light.

Einstein's equation ($E = mc^2$) meaning energy and matter can be transformed into each other through light.

Quantum physics explains that we are all linked to the universe through energy. Energy will flow where our attention / focus is directed.

Like attracts like!

Everything begins with a thought and thoughts become things.

Every invention began with a thought.

We have evolved with the ability of thought. If you worry about an issue, your negating thoughts combined with adverse feelings can create and manifest a negative circumstance.

If you are aware of such a circumstance, why not focus your energy into optimistic feelings and manifest positive outcomes?

Have you ever thought of someone and suddenly you bump into them or they phone you?

Have you listened to the radio and thought of a song then it's played on the radio? This is quantum physics at work.

We generate approximately 50,000-70,000 thoughts a day - possibly 35-48 thoughts per minute. By learning to filter thoughts, it's possible to create the life you desire with focus and mindfulness.

There is the outer world and the inner world.

The outer world is the world where we were taught by our parents, society and educational faculties on a dogma based on what they were taught.

The inner world is your inner being - which you really are. Who you were born to be!

If you are centred within your inner self /soul, everyday through rehearsal of true heartfelt intention, all magical results will manifest in tune to synchronicity of the universe to attract to you your desires.

Every experience you have had in your life has been drawn to you by your behaviour, belief, reaction and response resulting in personal emotional events.

Now you can change the direction of your journey through awareness, mindfulness, positive behaviour and positive response with daily practice.

We all have a chance in life that is frequently repeated but we just don't notice because life gets in the way!

Once you learn how to reset and reprogram your brain, you can easily achieve presented opportunities provided it is with true heartfelt intention and honesty.

All you need is to act when your instinct or inner self informs you having recognised an opening.

We have the ability to be a deliberate creator with this new found knowledge and enjoy the process.

Quote;

"Energy is the currency of the universe".

"When you 'pay' attention to something, you buy that experience.

So when you allow your consciousness to focus on someone or something that annoys you, you feed it to your energy, it reciprocates the experience of being annoyed".

"Be selective in your focus because your attention feeds the energy of it and keeps it alive. Not just within you but in the collective consciousness as well." ....Emily Maroutian.

2 PERSONALITIES AND
THE LAW OF ATTRACTION

*C*elebrities have not been successful just through pure luck!

Most have stumbled upon the law of attraction due to their genuine desire and passion to discover their true purpose in life and achieve their goals and dreams.

They have lived their lives effectively creating their lifestyle, achieving their purpose on their personal why's and how's, resulting in transmitting their positivity to others around them.

Many famous people have already spoken out about the Law of Attraction as seen in the film 'The Secret' by Rhonda Byrne and include Will Smith, Jim Carrey, Oprah Winfrey Denzel Washington and Arnold Schwarzenegger. Bob Proctor, Jack Canfield to name a few.

These people have evolved and developed their creativity in a multitude of ways as they are more in tune with their inner self and therefore ideas that have developed through their intuition.

3 INITIATION

*M*arch 2014

Since my new found awareness of the law of attraction in March 2014, my perspective of life has altered to accommodate the design that the universe corresponds in accordance to our thoughts, emotions, fears, desires and ambition.

I believe that in conceding to the law of attraction is similar to an 'initiation'.

It is a personal journey where along the way we gather experience, self awareness and life lessons.

I have learned to detach and delete my previously learned thoughts, beliefs and behaviours that no longer served me.

I learned to resurrect myself by introducing innovative positive thoughts which were in tune to my true self and have learned to transform myself by being loyal to my spirit / soul.

I have learned to support myself and others with true sincere intentions. In successfully passing my 'initiation' I have been rewarded with success in my health, my needs and the magic and miracles continue.

During this journey of study and practice, I realised there was no "instruction manual" available for a novice in pursuit of this knowledge and therefore decided to help beginners by writing this book.

Remember life is about fun, joy and happiness.

Enjoy your learning and development, work on reducing stress for yourself, and remember life is a gift to you! Enjoy the process and continue to read and practice.

We all have our own stories.

On reflection of my experience of the law of attraction, I became conscious that my first deliberate positive manifestation was when I was around 7years old.

My teacher was very concerned that my reading ability was not to the standard of my class mates and as a result she asked me to go to my older brothers' class for his assistance and as a result, my brother was mocked and made fun of.

My teacher advised my brother to inform my Mum about my lack of ability to read.

I was placed in a remedial class with around four others that were in same situation as me. My embarrassment of letting my family down made me resolve to do something about my reading skills.

With assistance from my brother and parents, I improved in my skills of reading.

On deliberation, I purposely acted to create a positive outcome with no knowledge of law of attraction but with focus and intent.

My alchemical journey consciously began on the day I received a knock on my door from two policemen who notified me that my parents who had been travelling as passengers in a taxi were involved in an accident and had been admitted to hospital.

At this time my parents were 68 years old and prior to the accident, they lived totally independent lives. Medical investigations indicated both parents had suffered many broken bones and cuts.

My immediate thoughts were of gratitude as they were both alive and being treated in hospital. The situation could have been much worse and strangely, I seemed to cope very calmly and positively having acknowledged the circumstances!

My Dad had a fractured collar bone and broken ankle, and later had to undergo amputation of the lower part of his leg.

My Mum had a laceration to her eyebrow that required a great deal of stitches, two broken wrists and a fractured pelvis.

They both spent 25 days in hospital after which it was decided by the Consultants that they be transferred to another hospital for rehabilitation. I requested they rehabilitate at home with my assistance as I was more than willing to perform this.

I was concerned that if they were to be rehabilitated in another hospital, their home may not be equipped for their return and that may conclude with their admission to a nursing home! And so it was deemed they go home.

After a total of 9 months that comprised of pain, suffering, and restricted mobility, through perseverance and conscious changes to our demeanours, we all eventually settled comfortably accepting the radical changes to our lives.

My job at that time was as a Support Practitioner for individuals in maintaining their home within the community. I'm so grateful for my knowledge and experience gleaned in this profession as it assisted my family in dealing with our circumstance.

During this episode of my life, I became overwhelmed with a feeling of gratitude and felt I had the strength and faith to cope with any situation positively. I had learned to see the world from a new perspective and this experience had shaken me to 'awaken me'.

Further revelations occurred at this time. While browsing through social media on the internet, my eyes were drawn to the words "The Secret" and "The Law of Attraction". In hindsight, this was no coincidence. This was the universe at work giving me universal winks and guiding me that would produce a multitude of synchronised events toward the needs for my parents in gaining a better quality of life!

Intrigued, I looked up these mysterious words and was lured into a new world of perception, life changing events and positive consequence.

Inspired, I sought out support groups, result groups and beginner groups. I monitored my thoughts and worked on re - programming myself. I learned through meditation to monitor my breathing, 1 no longer had panic attacks or heart palpitations. My breathing was controlled and I worked to remove mental blocks and resistance.

I met and celebrated with other student's on this path and discussed their results that were almost miraculous during which time I was introduced to my co-creating partner, Diane.

Having become a dedicated student of the law of attraction, I constantly studied, read, watched and listened to video teachings.
In meditation, I worked on my inner being, the source within where I established daily routines and practiced **Ho'oponopono** which is an ancient practice of appeasement and absolution. I made a gratitude journal, a vision board, an intention jar, and continued with my visualisation practices in the discovery of my inner being.

Conversely, 1 dissolved all negative emotions such as anger, jealousy, bitterness, and removed myself from gossip in the process of reprogramming my mind to positive thinking.

This had dramatic effect on me and I found myself in a state of joy and happiness. It became easier with practice of positive thinking, hope and trust within this, our universe.

I was finding solutions to every personal event and circumstance and learned to take responsibility for my own opinions, emotions and not allow negative comments, criticism or remarks affect me.

Mind my own business, and detach from other people's beliefs.

I focussed on my desires.

I attracted positive people and positive outcomes to my desires.

1 learned that through honesty with true intention from my heart, outcomes became better and better.

I learned that this state of joy and happiness is what begets everything you desire.

I studied the power of words and their significance, to state words, think words, speak words, text words and believe their meanings are achievable if it's done positively.

By training this way, I felt I was at the heart of the "vibration" of positive occurrence to people around me!

What you say to others can have such an impact whether positive or negative.

I now wake up each morning with excitement of a child as if it's Christmas morning each day.

I wake up with eagerness and ask the universe, "what magic today?"

With true heartfelt emotion there is neither judgement nor ego!

I aim for your journey through life to be of deserving joy.

4 GRATITUDE IS ATTITUDE

I am not religious!

From a young age, society and convention taught me religion is what your family teaches you!

Therefore my values were to respect my family's principles.

I grasped the meaning of music combined with lyrics through attendance at church with my Aunt Millie that filled me with the joy of music of hymns.

This is where my love for music and its many forms of composition and feeling began.

Moreover, it also contributed to my sense of humour, as when my brother accompanied me and although he adored the experience, he was always out of key! From these weekly forays, l empathised with the joy he had and learned not to judge at this very stage!

Who am I to judge?

Think about it! .....mmm this is where I truly learned that an individual can achieve happiness, from whatever they feel confident to do!

What makes us superior?

We are all born the same and we end the same! That is, there is one guarantee we all have in life, we all die.

We are all brothers and sisters but are encouraged and trained from the day we are born in our particular societies beliefs, rules and constraints.

l was born and immediately pushed onto the path of Catholicism. But as the years passed, I thought no! I want to find me!' I discovered Buddhism which I studied and loved it! From these beginnings, I learned to meditate. that yielded surprising innovations within my being.

l found me!

I discovered I could draw, paint, sing and write. Such a revelation. finding my inner self. Wow, it's amazing, and the true me / you is creative, inspiring and waiting to be released!

Considering religion, almost all Holy patriarchs give thanks to the "one" before he receiving substance. No matter what the "one" is, we are all linked to "it".

From my viewpoint, the universe loves and responds to gratitude. Gratitude increases and strengthens the frequency and vibrations your inner self. A person who lacks gratitude for what they have lose this wonderful gift.

I have witnessed and experienced on many occasions broken relationships, the loss of material items such as homes, jobs and other worldly possessions.

QUOTE;

"Whoever has will, be given more, and he will have abundance. Whoever does not have, even what he has will be taken from him".
(Gospel of Matthew in the holy scriptures)

Like attracts like and like a ripple in a pond, one action will beget another.

Negative words, thoughts and deeds bring more of these similar types of experience to the individual. A kind of nature that is born through a lack of appreciation and gratitude.

The less true and genuine appreciation you show, the worse your situations and circumstances become.

If you concede that you are a 'victim' of consequence, telling everyone how dire your circumstances are, loving the attention and doing nothing to help yourself or others involved, the universe responds with the same or similar action.

If you maintain you are a 'survivor' showing gratitude the universe will respond with the same or similar action.

My sons would laugh at me when I found a penny and thanked it when I picked it up. The more often I did this, the more money I was finding!

I found £5 notes!

This, I believe, was the universe responding to my openness and honesty.

There are benefits by practicing the act to pay it forward.

To freely give and receive will assist your positive development by causal actions - and it also feels good!

Methods of doing this can be as simple as smiling at people - in a friendly manner of course!

That one smile can instantly change a person's current outlook. Smiling is contagious.

A simple act of kindness by opening the door for someone can lift a person's mood. For example, standing in a queue and assisting someone that is struggling with their shopping bags.

Tipping a taxi driver or waitress, helping someone cross the road or up some stairs.

Give someone a compliment about their perfume or their hair.

Write a thank you card to people that have provided you with a service to show them that you took time out to thank them.

I am for ever making thank you cards as I get great pleasure that lifts my vibrations while enjoying the craft. I enjoy sending them to my friends for them to have the same experience in forwarding the cards onto their friends.

Offering to run an errand for someone elderly during the winter months.

Tidying your home and handing in your in unwanted items to a second hand shop. One man's junk is another man's treasure!

Hand in your used books or pass them onto Doctor's surgery, dentist or hospital waiting rooms.

All these examples display open appreciation.

We shouldn't consider the consequences of all these actions as a personal achievement. To do that would be self righteous and narcissistic. You do these deeds openly with consideration for others.

I was offered an opportunity to buy a ticket from a friend to attend the theatre as her circumstances at that time dictated she couldn't attend.

Although excited at this prospect, I didn't have the £40 for the ticket but knew within myself that it would appear.

The following day a remittance of £100 found its way to my purse.

l had the £40 to buy the ticket from my friend but unfortunately, my own circumstances changed and I couldn't attend!

I asked my friend if she knew someone who would appreciate the gift of this ticket and she suggested her daughter. I gave this freely as l manifested £100 through the desire to go and therefore had no regrets and no resistance to give it away as freely as it came to me.

As a result, the group of friends that attended the theatre, met the cast and I had the privilege of celebrating their experience. All is good!

Good things come from good.

5 EMOTIONS

*E*motion - the cause of so many actions!

Our emotions are a combination of psychological expressions, biological response and manifestation of action.

Being aware of our emotions can have a positive impact on decision making and goal planning.

Fear is the opposite to courage where as love is the opposite to hate.

Love is the essence of the soul which opens many gates to abundance.

Fear deprives the soul from evolving and promotes negative thoughts to multiply and manifest.

Our emotions affect our thoughts, that feed our emotion, which in turn manifests actions into reality.

Whether the end result are positive or negative depends on the universal response to your feelings.

Positive emotions lead to increased vibration energy that create positive manifestations.

Through this awareness, you will solutions to problems, intuitive actions, growth in confidence, and become in tune with creativity.

POSITIVE EMOTIONS:

Abundance of consciousness
Attitude of gratitude
Receiving graciously
Optimism
Contentment
Giving willingly
Wanting for others
Setting personal goals
Taking inspired action
Developing life plans
Being happy and content in your present circumstance
Embracing change
Continuously learning
Forgiving yourself and others for past mistakes
Allowing positive energy flow
Thinking positive thoughts
Expressing positive ideas
Celebrating others successes

NEGATIVE EMOTIONS:

Negative emotions can lead to ill health and negative circumstances that can be easily rectified by your awareness of your thoughts, feelings and behaviour and by working on your focus on positive goals.

Worrying
Boredom
Criticising behaviour
Holding a grudge
Having a sense of entitlement
Blame others for failures
Fear of change
Irritation and frustration
Know it all behaviour
Secretly hoping others fail
Wanting more

With awareness, you can monitor your mood and achieve the power and ability to create positive outcomes.

QUOTE:

"We do not attract what we want, we attract what we feel" (Ralph Smart)

We were born to have an enjoyable life.

We were not born to be miserable or unhappy. This type of condition depended on your parents actions! But you have the power within you to change this.

The universe wants you to feel joy and happiness as this is what aligns you to your positive evolution.

Each happy and joyful feeling is the true you. Your inner self. We are all exceptional souls with different demeanours due to our traditions, cultures and upbringing.

Actions we perform should bring us joy and positivity.

Learning of the law of attraction should be fun.

By participation in learning and understanding, your abilities can be developed to an inordinate capacity by undertaking such activities as writing, painting, arts and crafts, fishing, sailing, horse riding, dancing, learning a musical instrument, playing with your children, all types of self study and even jogging.

Once you discover the true you, your inner self, you will be astonished at how much you enjoy having these new abilities that will undoubtedly make you happy and give you great pleasure.

You will be amazed at how creative you become too!

Your confidence and belief in yourself will grow.

You will have the spark to lighten up a darkened room when you enter with your positive energy flowing to others.

As you go to bed each night, spare 5 minutes to reflect on what made you happy this day.

On reflection, you will experience that period of joy to sleep and awake the next day feeling positively refreshed to begin a chapter of your life.

Make a habit of doing this each night as part of your normal bedtime routine.

As an example, let's compare two individuals as an example of getting up in the morning.

If a person wakes up over sleeping their alarm for work, there is panic and anxiety at the beginning of their day that can result in their tights / stocking being laddered (if you wear these), bus / train running late or road works on the way to work.

The end result is a stress response that can carry throughout the day.

Conversely, if a person wakens up fresh with happy thoughts from the previous day, appreciates the smell of the fresh air, loving the sound of the birds singing or the rain on the window, smiling at the man waiting at the bus stop, the day has begun positively.

6 TRUE INTENTION

*T*rue intention is the most powerful force.

Selfless gratitude to all things increases the feelings in your heart.

You are now able to feel with true intention.

Be true to who you are. Know what you desire with your heartfelt intention whether it is negative or positive knowing that this is the result of what you will achieve and accept the consequences wholeheartedly.

By using your power of imagination, feel as if you already have that desire with your heart. Your intention will require the desired action that will manifest. Visualisation from imagination can be extremely powerful!

This is why it's important to monitor your focussed energy on positive intention. With true heartfelt intention is there should be neither ego nor judgement.

A happy contented life is complete while touching the heart of others.

QUOTE;
As witnesses not of our intentions but of our conduct, we can be true or false and the hypocrite's crime is that he bares false witness against himself. What makes it so plausible to assume that hypocrisy is the vice of vices, is that integrity can indeed excise under the cover of all vices except this one.

(Hannah Arendt)

We are all beings of vibration.

QUOTE; "All physical matters are composed of vibration".
Dr Max Planck

We acquire different levels of vibrations depending on our evolution, biological make up, and psychological development.

Einstein proved that when we break the matter down into smaller components, as the frequency and vibration of energy slows, we shift to a more material substance.

Take for example the three states of water - fluid (natural state), gas (steam), and solid (ice). Each vibrating at different frequencies.

If our emotions are of fear, despair, grief, anxiety, anger, bitterness, jealousy or any negative emotion, we affect our rate of thought vibration at a low frequency.

As a result we manifest negative results of those particular thoughts.

If on the other hand our emotions are of love, gratitude, joy, appreciation, happiness, celebrations, our vibrations are high, bringing more positive thoughts and producing comfortable manifestations.

Thought is the father of the deed!

When two frequencies are brought together, the lower frequency tends to rise to meet the higher attuning itself to the dominant frequency.

For example, if 3 people share a conversation and one is rather negative, the two positive conversations can change the negative conversation.

When your vibration is raised, you can generate the same effect on others around you. Can you imagine the world if all of us could achieve this harmony, peace and tranquillity.

This is why it's very important to be aware of positive thoughts, and positive speech. Thoughts become things.

Your subconscious is the other you.

Your subconscious contains everything you have ever experienced in your life but because we are only 1/10 conscious. You are not aware or have forgotten an amazing amount of facts, experiences and situations that are only triggered through word association, smells, music, and situations for example.

Cheerful memories can often be recalled where as bad memories are more commonly forgotten until something jogs it from its subconscious hiding place.

Many of these "bad" memories affect us as we mature and become part of our development making us highly sensitive and aware to certain situations and people without knowing how. A "gut feeling".

For example, your report from school is written "chatterbox", "easily distracted" and "daydreamer" can come up again in later life through discussion of your personal history that may trigger subconscious memories resulting in a profound effect on your psych.

When these realisations are presented to us, we should embrace them and work on changing our perception from existing in our old experiences to living in the our present in the pursuit of who we really are.

This is the law of deliberate creation. What you feel and what you think vibrate as a response to the use of the words.

Quote:
"The pen is mightier than the Sword" Edward Bulwer Lytton

An example of some powerful words used are "I am".

Quote:
I think therefore I am. Rene Descartes

From a psychological viewpoint, "I think therefore I am" relates to distinguishing a sentience and awareness when identifying a "thing" as a conscious entity.

Contrary to this when in the context of humans, and from a personal perspective, I am of the opinion that people who use this expression are selfish. "I am that person", "I am the only one that can do this"!

When I learned of how influential these little words actually are, I changed my belief and reprogrammed my understanding.

With the deliberate use of such words you are using your divine power affect your demeanour, character, ego.

Many people are happy to remain in their own comfort zone, not extending their limitations as they are content and safe without challenging themselves or their abilities. Yet, they know better than others - "I recognize I am better than you". A legend in their own world!

On the other hand, I know people who feel they are too old to study, to learn or develop. This causes barriers of development, evolution and lost opportunities.

We are always presented with a choice in our daily life and it's these preferences that lead to changes in circumstances and events in life's journey.

With this new found awakening we have an opportunity to release the old you and reinvent yourself.

If you think of past experiences where you have been wronged, avoid dwelling on it as these emotions return and feed the thought causing you to become upset.

Let it go!

Reset your mind and think positive thoughts to raise your vibration as the higher vibration will dominate your being with constant practice and awareness.

You can reset and reinforce your mind against these types of harmful attacks at any time you feel a negative thought presenting itself.

We have been programmed throughout our lives to accept that we have to work hard for money. Yet there is the old adage - "money is the root of all evil'.

Believe me - there is enough money in the universe to go around.

In your mind, change the word from "earning" and use the word "giving" with an open heart.

If you believe 'I can't afford' or 'I don't have enough' you are stopping or slowing your personal progress in the belief of your capabilities.

If you are struggling financially, deal with it! Arrange a financial payment plan for example and at least you be at some degree of ease that will enable you to continue your practice and release yourself from tension and stress.

Refrain from begrudging your debts and alternatively be grateful for the money you have already.

If you are treating yourself to new clothes feel and know you deserve them. This new perspective opens the door to you receiving more.

If you have in your mind "I will be happy when I have .....", or "It will never happen", are all negative foundations for further thoughts.

You have to think and bear positive connotations that it will attract personal enjoyment and pleasure therefore allowing the nature of everything else to fall in place.

If you're unhappy with your job then change it do something you enjoy doing.

When you are not ready to do something and feel you are being pushed, you will build a resistance.

I personally experienced this after my parent's accident.

My Mum developed severe anxiety (negative emotion) that culminated over a short period of time to her being unable to digest food that resulted in her losing four stones in weight.

Although I discussed this previously, this period of my life had a profound effect and acted on my intuition.

l was in the "right place at the right time" that enabled me to assist her.

She was taken to hospital where she was fed with the aid of a gastric tube inserted through her nostril to her stomach, This built her up and gave her energy to prepare her body to cope with surgery of her stomach which eventually cured her.

On her discharge, I was trained to feed her at home and my mum's stress and anxiety had a ripple effect on my coping with her management.

I had created my own resistance.

Having realised this, I decided to take a step back and arranged the district nurses to take over from me who were very good and Mum eventually gained enough weight and recovered fully.

This experience taught me to take responsibility for my negative actions and not to let them develop and grow.

If you feel your inner being is threatened by your own weakening behaviour, if circumstances allow, make alternative arrangements to allow time for your own spiritual first aid treatment.

7 LAW OF ATTRACTION TOOLS

$\mathcal{T}$here are many laws of attraction tools we can learn to use.

Enjoy the process of learning. Have fun doing every activity. Life is not meant to be a chore.

During my life's journey, I have learned the lesson of the dualities of conflict with negative and positive thoughts.

When I realised, I began to monitor my thoughts. 1 decided to wear an elastic band around my wrist to ping against my skin when I was having negative thoughts.

1 would 'STOP' and 'RESET' my thoughts to a happy thought that brought me joy that led to more positive thoughts.

This little ritual worked really well for me. So much so, that after three weeks of monitoring, I no longer required using the elastic band. I had re programmed my mind to think positive which meant when a problem manifested mentally, I was prepared to respond positively and found solutions so much more easily.

I began to respond rather than react!

During this time I began to write a daily gratitude journal.

I would write at least 10 things that I was grateful for each day and this helped the feeling within me to expand.

l would carry on during my day as normal and continue with grateful thoughts in my mind.

I found a pebble and declared it my *"gratitude rock"* which l kept in my bag.

l learned to do things that made me happy and brought me joy. l learned that this raised my vibrations immensely to the extent I gathered internal energy.

I learned to quiet my mind and meditate, control my breathing, exhaling negativity and inhaling positivity.

l began to ask the universe a question and learned to follow my intuition very quickly.

By using your imagination and visualisation on your question, playing it out in your mind along with strong positive emotion with your heart and using all your senses, you are creating a small world of your own making that with good intention may manifest.

The Vision Board

A "Vision Board" is an aid you can use to help your visualisation.

I used a board in the kitchen of my parents' home where I placed a few drawings and pictures:

There was a picture of my Dad walking as we intended on him learning to walk on a prosthetic leg after his amputation.

l had also did a pastel drawing of a grey coloured cat.

l also pinned on the board a picture of my mum looking vibrant and smiling as we longed for her to be well.

We walked past the board daily taking note and looking at it and astonishingly, it all manifested.

My Dad has his prosthetic leg, my Mum is looking fantastic and we have our beautiful cat Pasha.

The Creation Box

Another tool you can use is a "Creation Box".

Use and empty box and have fun decorating it whatever way you wish as this is your magic box which will be filled with your desires.

On the inside lid, write the words "whatever is contained in this box IS"! And so it's done!

When you feel your vibrations are up, write on a piece of paper what you desire on one side, and on the other write down why you desire it!

Cut out pictures of desires, places you would like to be, anything you wish to achieve!

For a *"Creation Jar"*, use an empty washed coffee or jam jar.

When you're feeling intuitive, write down on a piece of paper your intentions you would like to attract and place in the jar.

I fill this jar every so often and find that when I empty it every two weeks or so and read through them, I can dispose at least 8 pieces of paper as the intentions have already manifested. It feels amazing doing this and the more you see manifesting, the more trust you gain in the universe that is providing for you.

How about a *"Creation Journal"*?

This is the same idea as a vision board only you benefit by carrying it around with you where you can focus on the images contained more frequently.

The Past pretend game

This is where you write down an intended event as if it has already been done!

You do this with so much feeling while you write it, describing the smells, the sounds as you envisage it in its past tense, a week ago, a month ago, 2 months ago, a year ago for example.

I already have a book with previous imageries recorded and when I look back and read my entries and what has already manifest, it is incredible!

Gratitude money

This means what it says!

Write a thank you note that reads *"thank you so much for all of the money I have received throughout my life"* and attach it to a £5 note.

Place the money in your purse or wallet and read it occasionally with feeling of appreciation and gratitude and watch what happens!

The 52 week money challenge

This is intended to assist you in expanding your financial gain
Purchase a savings container and draw out a chart with 51 weeks on it.

In the column headings write:

Week	Deposit	Balance

Begin in week 1 by depositing £1
Week 2 - £2 = £3.
Week 3 - £3 = £6 and so on until on your week 52 - £52 that will equal a total of £1378.00.

This helps open the acceptance of money into your life and assists in the maintenance of a positive cash flow.

Feel good, be happy and enjoy your life.

These are the simple instructions to follow to get you into alignment of the universe and of your desire. By believing and being open and honest to yourself, you are able to achieve your manifestations and your desires.

You are in alignment when you believe. You can be at ease and enjoy the process of your development and your journey with anticipation of what's to come and the knowledge that it is already in existence.

Avoid questioning of how it will come about and manifest.
You are not in alignment when your focus is on the need and want of it!

"Why has it not manifested yet?"

"What am I doing wrong?"

Just believe and receive!   Go with the flow!

Let it go and enjoy the process.

To be in tune, to be in harmony, the order of vibration.

The more consciously aware we become of ourselves and all that surrounds us, the higher our frequency becomes.

When you are free from the negative obstructions in your mind and able to flow freely, you become inspired and confident to take action.

Look at a child that has yet to conform to the traditions and culture of its environment. He or she plays, speaks and acts freely always inquisitive with no inhibition.

Like this child, you begin to attract the people, and events through synchronicity with the universe.

I believe there is no such thing as coincidence. When you become aligned and free of blockages in your psyche, you attract synchronised events that offer opportunities for your desires. Opportunities arise and it's your decision to choose which action to take to manifest which result.

The more you are in tune with your intuition, the more confident you become. It is then when like attracts like and you may find you attract people to your desires.

When you act on your intuition you have made your decision with trust that can lead to the next synchronised event

8 AFFIRMATIONS

I am a failure!

In raising your awareness, important to rid yourself of old and conventional beliefs such as - I can't, it's impossible, it's not achievable, and, 1 am a failure, for example. These types of negative attitudes attract the same or similar feelings within your own being. Everything is possible and achievable. This is your subconscious directing and trying to govern you.

In order to delete these, you apply daily affirmations throughout your day. This routine will affect a change in your perception positively that can increase your confidence and when you begin to see the results, it will reinforce your conviction in the universe. This is the law of deliberate creation working hand in hand with your feelings and your vibration. By repeating the following affirmations you may begin to feel and actually experience that you are living the affirmations. This is you using your divine power within to create your divine plan!

The most powerful words in their positive sense to utilise in this process are "1 am........."

1 am attracting positive people and positive events to my desires.
1 am open to receive and give freely.
1 am success.
1 am responsible for my feelings.
1 am healthy.
1 am love.
1 am prosperous.
1 am divine.
1 am fused with the universe.
1 am at ease.
1 am clear in the direction toward my desires
1 am attracting positive solutions.

This power comes with the repetition of the affirmations. The key is to feel what the affirmation portrays deep within your emotional self. Respond rather than react which will adjust your behaviour accordingly to any event that may arise.

QUOTE:

"We achieve inner health only through forgiveness- the forgiveness not only for others but also ourselves"
Joshua Loth Liebman

You are a reflection of your subconscious.

To be open and allow positive aspects become attracted to your life, it's good to work on forgiveness of yourself initially.

Old routines of beguile and resentment, jealousy and bitterness are common negative sentiments that have to be forgiven and let go!

They are created by you and are a reflection of your character, a mirror of what you created, and a reflection of your subconscious.

On elimination of this influence of your own design, you will discover a surge of reconciliation within your own being.

The following examples will aid to clear harmful and damaging memories that are manifesting your problems. Forgiveness sets you free!

By ignoring the ability to change within you toward a greater good may cause resistance and prevent your own personal development.

For example, past broken relationships and the memories that is bound to this period. Put time aside when you are alone to recall and think about them. Use forgiveness within you to and work on letting go them go! Don't carry them around for the rest of your life.

You may discover why you are not moving forward!

9 HO'OPONOPONO

*T*his is an ancient Hawaiian mantra used by the Kahuna, the mystic healers who have been around for centuries.

Prayers and Mantra's help you accept full responsibility for circumstance, past relationships or situations while you are healing yourself and endeavour to improve your world and all around you.

You are a mirror and whatever you manifest will be reflected in your actions. The Mantra is a way of problem solving with repentance and forgiveness....'forgive and you shall be forgiven'

Try the following for yourself:

1. Close your eyes and imagine anyone you would like to heal - including yourself, or to help mend a relationship or memories which previously troubled you.

2. Repeat these four phrases with true heartfelt intention:

    I am sorry

    Please forgive me

    I love you

    I thank you

By repeating 'l am sorry' and 'please forgive me' you are asking your divine self to forgive you for your response that brought these circumstances to you.

By saying and feeling 'thank you' and 'I love you' you are reconnected to your divine self.

Flowing with energy through you, freeing blockages allowing you to notice synchronised events and situations that make it easier for you to take action on new presented opportunities.

A BUDDIST PRAYER FOR FORGIVENESS

If I have harmed anyone in any way either knowingly or unknowingly through my own confusion, I ask their forgiveness.

If anyone has harmed me in any way through their own confusion I forgive them unconditionally.

If there is a situation where I am not ready to forgive, I forgive myself for this.

For all the ways I harm myself, negate, doubt, belittle myself, judge or be unkind to myself through my own confusion, I forgive myself.

FORGIVENESS PRAYER

The Divine Creator, Father, Mother, Son are one.

If I, my family, relatives and ancestors have offended you, your family, relatives and ancestors in thoughts, words, deeds, we ask your forgiveness.

Let this cleanse, purify, liberate from all negative memories, obstructions, energies and vibrations and transmute these unwanted energies to pure light.

DAILY ROUTINES

Begin you day by setting your alarm five or ten minutes early to begin your positive thoughts by lying there and feeling relaxed.

The positive aspect of this routine reduces stress and contributes to a feeling of calm and ease as your day unfolds.

During this 10 minute period, plan ahead how you intend your day by segmenting it and including things like how you hope that phone call to be, how happy your work colleagues are in the office.

As you continue with your washing and dressing as you arise in the morning, continue those happy positive thoughts as it only takes 17 seconds of a positive created in the mind to manifest.

Share; pre-plan your ideal car parking space, the traffic lights correspond to your smooth running, have positive thoughts of your bus arriving on time. If you're going shopping, pre-plan the items you desire to purchase and you may find that as your vibrations are raised and you're in alignment, all the items you wish to purchase are reduced or are on special offer that adds to the increased feeling of gratitude and appreciation that will attract more good feelings.

Expand that thought. From your imagination and visualisation, feel, smell, touch and believe it's real and done! If you are driving to your destination, play uplifting music that elevates your mood that helps keep your momentum flowing positively.

Throughout your day, try to spend 10 or 20 minutes meditating. This is an excellent habit to still your mind and ask yourself questions that can be revealed to you.

Through your love within, be as considerate, compassionate and as helpful as you possibly can by assisting those around you. You can do this by opening doors, smiling or assisting someone with their bag.
These are gestures that can have such an impact on that individual's day and could positively change their mood.

Conversely, the gesture may make you feel delighted and will raise your positive emotion. Try to spare 5 minutes writing in your gratitude journal by recording what you are grateful for now and what you intend to be grateful for.

Learn to appreciate and feel gratitude for your surroundings, fresh air we breathe, our senses, birds chirping, hot water, electricity, a roof over our head, blue sky. Appreciate the freedom to feel the wet and cold rain on your skin from the universe.

We are so blessed with so much that we never noticed.

We have the privilege of sharing the air that was one breathed by many famous composers, artists, poets, authors and musicians.

How fortunate are we!

Einstein was known to repeat the words 'thank you' up to 100 times each day. By doing this with feeling we connect to our intuition, mind and soul and that more ahaaaaaaa and ideas occur.

Before you go to bed to settle at the end of the night, spare a thought of what made you smile or happy today!

What achievement did you accomplish?

What solution did you discover?

Re-produce that feeling recalling when it happened and re – live that emotion. This assists you to rest easy knowing you accomplished something. It will convey a sense of ease and enthusiasm for tomorrow. You will awake the next day feeling good to continue you're routine.

Dedicate yourself to learning something new.

The more you become a dedicated student of your inner self, the more positive results appear to manifest and increasing positive results you may witness gaining trust in the response of the universe.

The more trust you gain, the easier it becomes to manifest your desires.

If you over sleep your alarm calls, monitor your responses during the day.

Assess your behaviour. If you react negatively, negative situations may arise.

So stop.

Restart at any time and begin to respond positively. Life is far too short for stress.

Enjoy your journey!

10 INSPIRED ACTION

*W*hen you work on your inner self, learn to trust and grow in confidence.

When you are in a place of joy and happiness, your thoughts connect to your emotions and feelings bringing it all together with your inner being /soul.

You discover intuition, gut feelings, and then magic happens. Ideas pop into your head and you experience the "AHAAAA" moments!

This is where an impulsive act at an unexpected moment occurs that feels right.

Pay attention and be alert to take inspired action. If it feels good and you enjoy it, the universe will orchestrate the next chain of events for your manifestations and desires.

This is where you are inspired to take action immediately.

It's as if Divine intervention needs your response.

Opportunities fall at our feet frequently and we never noticed them or have failed to act upon them. This is the universe communicating to us through universal nudges and winks.

I personally have had amazing results when I act on inspired action on many occasions.

I compare this to following the Yellow Brick Road.

There's no frustration or impatience whilst acting on it.

You are merely priming a pump to allow the universe to take over and let more opportunities arise.

Remember, one response can cause a ripple effect on other outcomes.

DRIFTWOOD

Driftwood is when the universe nudges or winks at you to pay attention as it is acknowledging your aspiration and focus / energy spent.

It's letting you know it's on its way to you.

If for example, your focus is on travel / holiday and you are aware of the advertising and destinations you desire, all of a sudden competitions for you to enter may result with a positive outcome.

This is working with your vibrations to align you to your desire. When you take notice of these synchronisations, you increase your sensations with trust, knowing a positive outcome is on its way.

It's now up to you to trust and use inspired action. If you look back on your relationships for your request for your soul mate / ideal partner, take note of the qualities you wished for in that person.

If the manifested relationship resulted in not being your perfect request, analyse the qualities you don't like and you may find that these qualities in your partner are the result of the fears or negative aspirations you didn't pay attention to, there by attracting that person.

1 have been married and divorced twice in my life, both men were alcoholics.

Although they had certain positive qualities that I desired, my fear and negative vibration attracted alcoholic traits leading to undesirable behaviour.

The lessons I learned directed me to the job of working with people who had alcohol dependency and people who had mental health issues.

The universe has a sense of humour!

BE CAREFUL WHAT YOU WISH FOR!

When you begin to focus on your desires, it's important to deliberate on only good intentions as you would not want to cause harm to anyone in the process.

If your focus is on wealth, it is very beneficial to include the words 'tranquillity', 'harmony' and 'peace'.

It will provide reassurance to you that no harm will come to anyone around you during the process.

The universe has a very good – cryptic sense of humour. Therefore, in your deliberations, be as specific as you possibly can.

When I was studying and practicing the law of attraction, I began to experiment and during this period, I smoked cigarettes.

I once wished for gold for my birthday, meaning gold jewellery. Gold was exactly what I received from my brother!

My mouth dropped in amazement when he handed a beautiful lighter in the shape of a gold nugget with the words GOLD written on the front!

Even more amazing were the words 'made in the universe' inscribed n the back!

I was so grateful for this gift and amazed at the working of the universe!

I therefore thanked the universe and my brother as my belief was even more reinforced and I was eager to experiment more.

This leads me to a story I wish to share with you regarding real driftwood!

Prior to my studies and knowledge of law of attraction, I was responsible for the safety of three men on a sea dive.

On our way to our destination, I had noticed a very large piece of driftwood floating in the water.

The weather had been stormy the previous week resulting in this piece of wood probably being dislodged with all sorts of other things from the sea.

We arrived at our diving destination and the three men began donning their gear for their diving adventure. Once under the water, they would normally spend on average 20 minutes for their dive.

I would sit aboard the Rib (Rigid Inflatable Boat), and my normal routine would be to observe for the first sign of bubbles appearing on the surface of the water then prepare to help them on board the rib.

On this day when they made their dive, a strong wind picked up. The rib was blown around and drifted so quickly I suddenly became disoriented. This is sometimes known as sea blindness.

l had no idea where I was, where the divers were and obviously I panicked.

I literally had to talk myself out of this state of fear and calmly I began to breathe in and out slowly. The thoughts that ran through my head were obviously of the safety of the men, one of which was my partner.

It was my responsibility to find them and get them on board safe and well.

I focussed and prayed for a sign to locate them and suddenly I noticed something very far ahead on the surface of the water.

l thought is this one of the men so I started the engine of the boat and headed toward him.

As I got close, I noticed it was a piece of driftwood we had passed on our way to the diving site.

I realised l must be close to the divers and slowed the engine down when I saw the three figures in the water waving for my attention.

I was so grateful to see them, so appreciative to drag them on board, and I was also so apologetic! Thankfully, they were all good natured, calm and understanding.

Many lessons were learned that day.

Driftwood may be debris but in this instance, it was most definitely valuable and provided me with a very deep seated life experience.

In reflection, l paid attention. I followed my intuition to track the driftwood I had previously seen and my awareness resulted in a happy ending!

Thank the universe!

Sometimes the universe orchestrates dilemmas!

There is great power in our thoughts, words spoken and written. They can be used negatively or positively to attract you such as seen in advertising.

Sometimes the universe orchestrates dilemmas or obstacles that we have to counter positively to overcome. This means that a change is on its way and by adjusting your attitude from victim to survivor, positive outcomes are maintained.

Responding positively rather than reacting negatively changes behavioural patterns and attracts positive circumstances. Change your story by using positive words and speak of how you wish the outcome to be.

When my parents were rehabilitating, people would ask me of their progress. Although we were experiencing obstacles, I would take the improved situations into account and discuss this rather than the downbeat aspects.

This behaviour shifted our position to better experience influences on our thoughts and emotions to a higher frequency which again attracted more positive experiences to us.

If people spoke negatively, I would direct the conversation onto a positive mode that would change other people's perspective of our conversation positively.

If you are discussing your situation through complaining about how you don't want it to be only adds to that current experience and attracts more aspects that will align to the situation!

When I encounter this, I ask, "so what do you want?" Or, "what would be your desired outcome?"

This helps to change their perspective and contributes to shifting positively.

11 BRING IT ALL TOGETHER

*Y*ou have the power to create your own story!

With commitment and regular practice, you can achieve the life you desire by repetitive reading of this book using all of the aforementioned tools.

You have the power to create your own story and paint your own picture of how you wish your life to be. With use of all of the tools provided you will discover the true you, this divine person inside.

As your confidence and trust grows, your belief in the universe will nurture bringing with it, freedom from anxiety and depression.

You will feel that you can attract optimism and encouragement in all that surrounds you but it's important to accept responsibility for your own feelings and emotions and not be drawn into other people's dramas.

That is the chronicle of their life that is being written as they talk, behave and react to all that is around them.

Do not worry about what other people think of you. Whatever you emanate will attract back to you the same therefore; why not focus all of your energy on your dreams, goals and positive emotion!

Enjoy the journey and have fun in the process. You were born as a unique individual who deserves to have a fun filled active prosperous life!

Go for it! What have you got to lose?

Avoid the need or the wants in life.

Ask, believe and receive with in precision of your feelings, true heartfelt intentions, connecting your mind, heart and soul. It's done!

Breathe as if you have it with passion.

Avoid the need or the want.

Feel the success that is already here as when you do this and focus, it will be on its way.

Do not question how it will appear, or what do you have to do. Your intuition will guide you when to act, what phone calls to make, and set in motion the wheels of action.

Step back and trust all synchronised events that bombard you as good or bad – these as for your own development and understanding.

You may at times experience a gap in your trust.

Reassert yourself, believe that what is happening at that moment will work in your favour....then the tipping point will arrive.

It's up to you now to act when your intuition tells you to!

As a result of your dedication in maintaining your routines and continually developing by learning law of attraction daily, you will flow with the law of attraction.

You will see results that will raise your vibrations over and over.

You will experience synchronisations of people, places, events and circumstances entering your life.

It's up to you now to act when your intuition tells you.

Your belief and trust will let it flow to you.

You will experience occurrences in your favour.

Continue helping others and celebrating their success as you are the heart of that vibration and circumstance.

Divine intervention will intercede at the correct moment filling you with the need to celebrate.

You are success and you deserve it all!

I love you and wish you to enjoy your journey shinning your light to all you connect to.

Thank you for allowing me to connect to you.

I am grateful.

ABOUT THE AUTHOR

Joanne Lowey has had 20 years experience working within various community institutional settings supporting children, adolescents, elderly, and individuals with mental health issues and alcohol dependency.

Joanne has made it her mission to motivate individuals toward accomplishing their positive, advantageous and constructive desires through their progress in life.

website: www.howtoflowwithlawofattraction.com

Printed in Great Britain
by Amazon

35531484R00032